DRIVING
QUESTIONS ANSWERED

by
Sallie Walrond, LHHI

Illustrations by
Carole Vincer

KENILWORTH PRESS

First published in Great Britain by
Kenilworth Press Limited,
Addington, Buckingham, MK18 2JR

© Kenilworth Press Limited 1995
Reprinted 1997, 2002, 2004

All rights reserved. No part of this publication
may be reproduced, stored in a retrieval system, or
transmitted in any form or by any means, electronic,
mechanical, photocopying, recording or otherwise,
without the written permission of the publisher.

British Library Cataloguing in Publication Data
A catalogue record for this book is available from the British Library.

ISBN 1-872082-80-7

Typeset by Kenilworth Press Limited

Printed in Great Britain by Westway Offset

CONTENTS ▪▪▪▪▪▪▪▪▪▪▪▪▪▪▪

DRIVING
QUESTIONS
ANSWERED

4 Introduction
5 Types of carriage
7 Springing
8 Vehicles for beginners
9 Correct fitting of vehicle
   for horse
12 Correct fitting of vehicle
   for driver
13 Problems
13 Napping
14 Sore shoulders
16 Fear of traffic
17 Driving in company
18 Refusing to stand still
20 Pulling
21 Eventing
22 Showing considered
24 Conclusion

Introduction

Growing interest in driving has resulted in the demand for carriages exceeding the supply, with century-old vehicles becoming harder to find. However, a new generation of carriage builders is now producing some superb vehicles, constructed with great expertise using modern materials. Sadly, there are also some new vehicles that are not as good and which may cause difficulties for inexperienced newcomers.

The choice of the type of carriage to be bought depends largely on the purpose for which it is needed. Beginners are frequently bewildered by the variety of carriages which are now available. It is sensible to seek expert advice before spending too much money on equipment. It is so easy to buy in a fit of enthusiasm and regret later.

It is essential that the carriage should fit the horse or pony, and in the case of a two wheeler that it should balance properly so that the animal is able to work comfortably and efficiently. It is also vital that his harness is correctly fitted. This is already explained in *Starting to Drive*, No. 28 in this series.

The horse must also be carefully trained so that he is not afraid and fully understands what is required so that he can co-operate with his driver.

Problems with harness horses and ponies, as with ridden animals, are usually initially created by man. Equines are frequently very long-suffering and will often tolerate pain inflicted by their well-meaning owners.

Horses have extremely good memories, though, and never forget the discomfort of ill-fitting and badly balanced vehicles or of uncomfortable harness, and small problems can easily develop into major catastrophes.

Types of carriage

Newcomers are often worried by the array of names that are given to carriages but they are not nearly as complicated as they first appear. It has to be remembered that, in the nineteenth century, carriages were often built to specification. They were likely to be given a name which referred to the designer, builder, body type, purpose for which they were used, or area in which they first appeared. This, today, can cause great confusion when people try to give names to old carriages.

It is easiest to put carriages into simple categories.

Governess carts are sometimes known as Tub Carts. It is quite likely that the beginner to driving, when looking for his first carriage, may be tempted to buy a Governess cart with a view to restoring it and eventually selling it at a large profit.

This can be an expensive mistake. The cost of professional restoration can run into vast sums of money as many of these vehicles need extensive work to make them roadworthy. They can also be hard to sell owing to the fact that the Whip has to sit in the rear right-hand side, at an angle, which allows very little purchase with the feet making the control of a pulling animal difficult. Also the entry and exit by the rear door can create problems with anything but the quietest animal. Of course, a Governess cart is ideal for taking small children out for quiet drives as once the children are in, and the door is shut, they are safe from falling out. The body was often hung low, between full elliptic springs, on a cranked axle, in order to give good springing and to keep the centre of gravity low for safety.

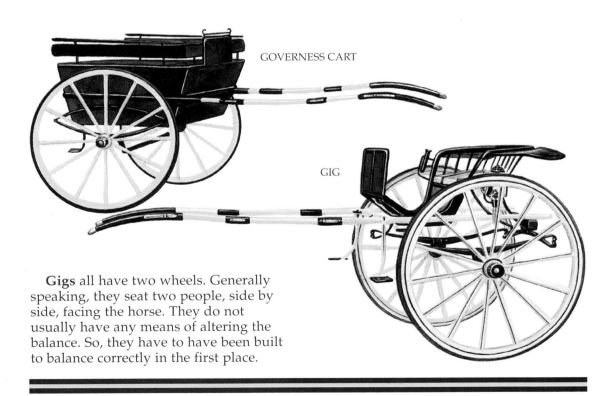

GOVERNESS CART

GIG

Gigs all have two wheels. Generally speaking, they seat two people, side by side, facing the horse. They do not usually have any means of altering the balance. So, they have to have been built to balance correctly in the first place.

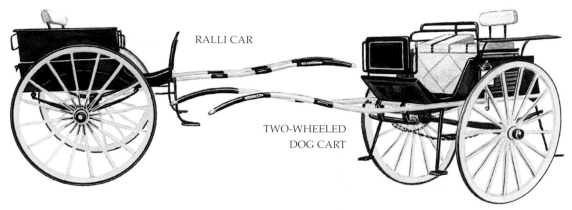

RALLI CAR

TWO-WHEELED
DOG CART

Dog carts and Ralli cars (not carts) can have either two or four wheels. They often have back-to-back seating with space under the seats for carrying dogs for sporting purposes. The difficulty of trying to carry passengers on the rear-facing back seats of two-wheeled dog carts is that even when the front seats are slid forward, it is still difficult to counteract the weight of rear-seat passengers, so only light children can be carried. It is far easier to have a four-wheeled dog cart when the weight of the rear-seat passengers is of no consequence to the balance. Four-wheelers do not have to balance like two-wheelers. The weight,

of course, must be considered in relation to the animal providing the motive power. **Waggonettes** serve the same purpose for carrying passengers but have inward facing rear seats. These vehicles are ideal for activities such as taking families on picnics.

Phaetons always have four wheels and come in many shapes and sizes. They are designed to be driven by the owner.

Landaus, Victorias and Broughams are all suitable to be driven by coachmen and are now favoured for weddings.

Coaches and Breaks are heavier four-wheeled vehicles for use with more than one horse.

FOUR-WHEELED DOG CART

WAGGONETTE

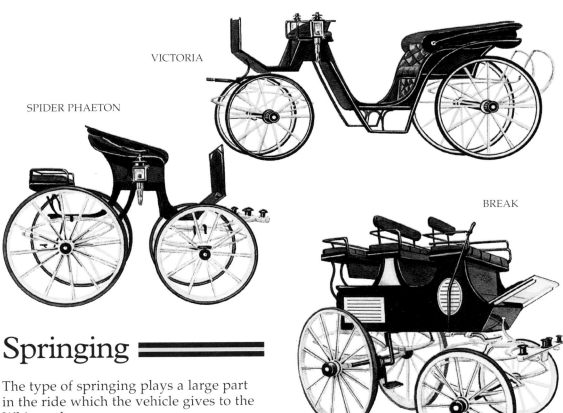

VICTORIA

SPIDER PHAETON

BREAK

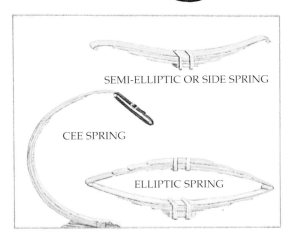

Springing

The type of springing plays a large part in the ride which the vehicle gives to the Whip and passengers.

Cee springs give a superb ride. Very often, these are combined with other springs and the carriage will ride like a Rolls Royce.

Both full elliptic and semi-elliptic springs also give a comfortable ride.

There are some modern vehicles, primarily designed for horse driving trials, which have very hard springing of special design. This is excellent for the purpose to which these vehicles should be put. In cross-country driving, soft springing can result in the driver and groom getting bounced out of the vehicle. However, hard springing is not recommended for anyone who suffers from back problems.

SEMI-ELLIPTIC OR SIDE SPRING

CEE SPRING

ELLIPTIC SPRING

Vehicles for beginners

There are numerous carts being built on pneumatic-tyred wheels and sold as suitable for beginners to drive. Some of these have been built by enthusiasts as a 'one off' and care must be taken before spending too much on such a cart which may turn out to be less than satisfactory.

One disadvantage can be the inability to balance correctly so that there is either too much weight on the pony's back, which makes the work a lot harder as he has to carry the vehicle as well as pull it, and this can result in a sore back through pressure from the saddle via the back band from the shaft tugs. Or there may be too much weight on the pony's girth area caused by upward pressure from the belly band via the shaft tugs. This can make a small pony feel as though he is almost being lifted off the ground. Such a vehicle also gives an unpleasant ride to the driver as 'knee rock' is created with every trotting stride.

Some carts are built without a seat rail at the back and side. This is highly dangerous as there is the likelihood of sliding off the seat and falling onto the road.

Some do not have enough leg room for an adult, and the Whip is forced to sit with his knees pressed against the dash board.

Some have the scaffold-pole-type shafts extending past the entry to the body and these have to be negotiated when getting in and out making entry difficult and dangerous.

Small wheels can make the vehicle difficult to balance when going up and down hills and also harder for the animal to pull as every mound appears to be steeper than with larger, carriage-type wheels.

There are, however, some exercise carts on pneumatic tyres which many people find quite satisfactory for everyday use. They are being made by builders who have plenty of experience of what is required to satisfy the needs of their customers.

It is a mistake, though, to spend too much money on a pneumatic-tyred cart when it may be sensible to spend a bit more and buy a vehicle built on carriage-type wheels to a more traditional design.

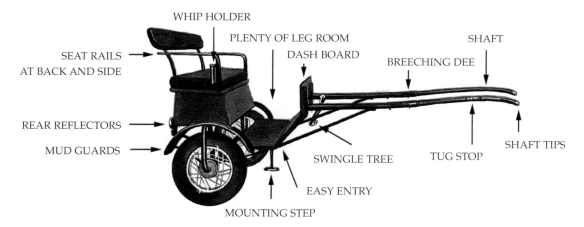

WHIP HOLDER

PLENTY OF LEG ROOM

SHAFT

SEAT RAILS
AT BACK AND SIDE

DASH BOARD

BREECHING DEE

REAR REFLECTORS

MUD GUARDS

SHAFT TIPS

SWINGLE TREE

TUG STOP

EASY ENTRY

MOUNTING STEP

LATE TWENTIETH-CENTURY EXERCISE CART

Correct fitting of vehicle for horse

It is important that the vehicle is of the correct size for the animal.

The shafts should lie lightly in the tugs. One which is too large will slope down-wards and one which is too small will slope upwards. When the vehicle is held with the seat level, the shafts should rest lightly in the tugs when the tugs are level with the swell (widest part of the side panel) of the saddle.

When looking at a vehicle it is a good idea to get someone to hold the shafts to enable you to mount, without the horse put to, and with the vehicle held level, see if it balances correctly. A measurement can be taken from the tug stop to the ground. This can be compared with the measurement taken when the horse is wearing the saddle, with the shaft tug level with the swell. This is a helpful guide when seeing a vehicle without being able to try the horse for height. If the seat is not level then the vehicle will not fit the horse.

VEHICLE TOO SMALL

VEHICLE TOO LARGE

VEHICLE LEVEL

Measure from tug stop to ground

The length and width of the shafts are important. If they are too short, there will not be enough room between the horse's hind quarters and the dash board for him to carry his tail comfortably.

Some animals will put up with this discomfort, but less charitable animals may understandably kick if put to such a vehicle. Short shafts are also likely to dig into the horse's shoulders or even get under the collar when a tight turn is negotiated. If the shafts are too long the horse may receive a dig in his neck when turning, or the rein may get caught round the end. Both can result in the horse refusing to turn sharply because he remembers the pain inflicted by the shaft when he turns.

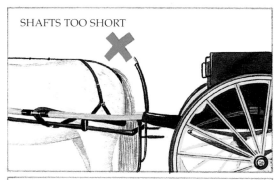

SHAFTS TOO SHORT

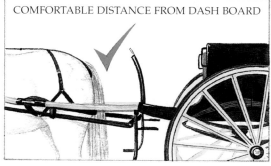

COMFORTABLE DISTANCE FROM DASH BOARD

SHAFTS TOO LONG

SHAFTS TOO SHORT

Too long – a shaft end is caught in the rein bringing the horse to the right and resulting in a loss of steering.

Too short – a shaft end is caught under the collar and is digging into the neck causing pain to the horse.

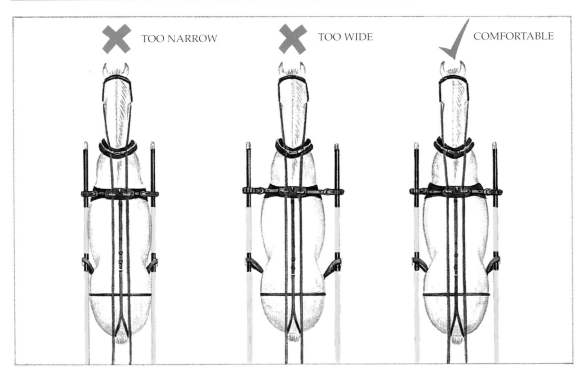

TOO NARROW ✗   TOO WIDE ✗   COMFORTABLE ✓

If the shafts are too narrow, the animal's sides will quickly get chafed and in extreme cases can even become raw. Shafts which are too wide allow the horse to swing about between them, and with some horses there could be a tendency for the hindquarters to be carried to one side.

This applies more to young horses who have not yet learnt to go absolutely straight than to mature animals who know their job.

Reining back would be more difficult with a young horse in such a vehicle.

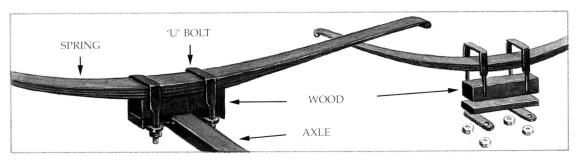

SPRING   'U' BOLT   WOOD   AXLE

Some vehicles will be found to have blocks of wood between the axle and the springs in order to make the vehicle higher.

These can be removed to lower the carriage. Equally, if necessary, blocks can be added to raise the vehicle a little.

Correct fitting of vehicle for driver

There are numerous carriages which do not have enough leg room for the average adult Whip. This is a grave disadvantage, because a comfortable and safe driving position cannot be obtained.

The driver should be able to sit on the box with his legs sloping down at a comfortable angle to enable him to gain firm purchase against the floor. If he is forced to drive with his knees bent so that his thighs slope upwards from the hips to the knees, forcing his feet to be tucked back underneath his legs, he will have great difficulty in controlling a troublesome horse.

It is just as dangerous for a small person to try to drive a carriage which is too large so that his feet hardly reach the floor. If the horse should pull hard, the Whip is likely to get hauled off the seat. A foot rest, built to the correct angle, to suit the driver, can solve this problem.

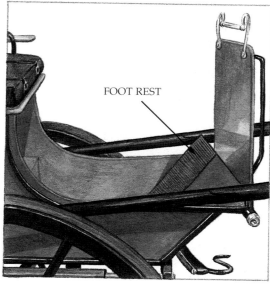

FOOT REST

A movable but firmly secured foot rest can be added to give a feeling of safety and security to a short-legged driver who is not able to reach the floor.

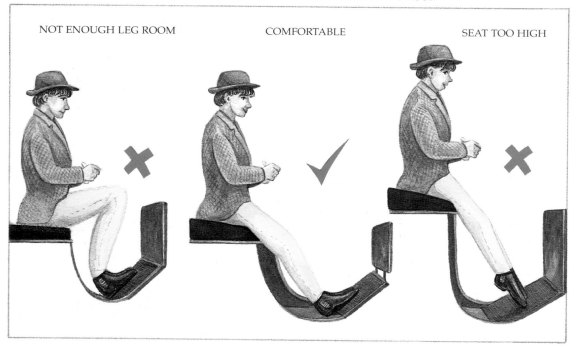

NOT ENOUGH LEG ROOM   COMFORTABLE   SEAT TOO HIGH

Problems

Having got the horse, the harness and the vehicle, the beginner is faced with getting on with the driving and sometimes problems arise through inexperience. Generally speaking, horses are willing to please as long as they understand what is required. Misunderstandings, though, can easily be mistaken for naughtiness. Horses learn by constant repetition and praise when they do things well.

Obviously, they must be corrected instantly if they wilfully disobey but tempers must **never** be lost. Nothing is ever gained from the driver losing his temper with an animal. This will probably result in the horse becoming confused and may even sour him for the rest of his life.

Napping

Horses may nap and refuse to go forward for a variety of reasons. Some will jib and refuse to move in any direction, others will rear, and some will plunge and throw themselves into their collars, and extreme cases may lie down. The initial cause must be analysed if the horse behaves in this manner.

One reason for napping can be caused by taking the horse for a drive and then, instead of going on a circular route, turning round in the road, after a mile or so, and coming home again. Such practice can result in the horse wanting to turn for home earlier and earlier until he eventually refuses to leave the yard.

It is vital always to have a purpose for the turn if a circular route is not possible. The whole idea is purely psychological but it does prevent problems – and it is always less trouble to prevent problems than to cure them.

JIBBING

REARING

LYING DOWN

Sore shoulders

Another cause of napping could be sore shoulders. Many people imagine that unless there is actually a visible sign such as bleeding or a pink, sore, patch under the collar, their horse does not have sore shoulders. In fact, a horse can suffer considerably from sore shoulders with very little to show to the inexperienced eye.

Reasons for sore shoulders can be:
- Lack of fitness and too much work before the skin on the shoulders has been given time to harden by increasing the work gradually. Horses must be given time. So often people are in too much of a hurry.
- Too heavy a load before the shoulders have hardened.
- An ill-fitting collar.
- A breast collar being used without a swingle tree but with fixed trace hooks.

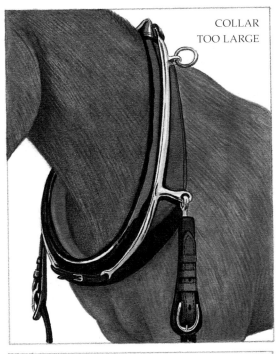

COLLAR TOO LARGE

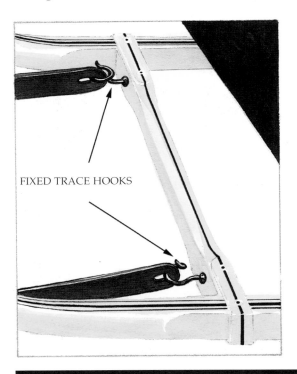

FIXED TRACE HOOKS

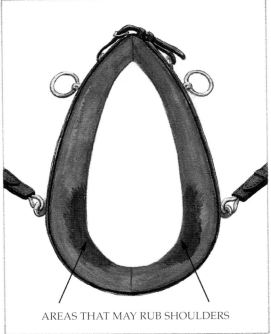

AREAS THAT MAY RUB SHOULDERS

● A dirty lining to a collar or one which has become worn out and has cracks or holes in the lining.

A careful watch must always be made for any sign of sore shoulders. When the horse is brought back from work, there may be damp patches on such areas as under the saddle, behind the ears and under the collar. The horse will usually be rubbed down and probably left to have some food. If, on returning an hour or so later, it is noted that the damp patches behind the ears and under the saddle have dried but those on the shoulders remain damp, the horse has probably got the beginnings of sore shoulders. These wet patches may still be visible the following day and can go on for the best part of a week before they dry completely.

The ignorant or unobservant person will not notice these sore areas and will happily put the same collar onto the horse the following day and ask him to work. The pain eventually becomes so extensive that the horse is forced to resist working in any way he finds to be effective. Once he has discovered that by jibbing, he can avoid the pain created by working he is likely to pursue the habit. He may then be punished and the results are inevitable. He will associate working with pain and will probably be ruined for life, as far as harness work is concerned.

The knowledgeable and caring person will spot the warnings of sore shoulders, investigate the cause and make sure it does not recur. The horse will be rested from being driven until his shoulders have hardened and hardening lotion will be applied repeatedly to hasten this. If the correct steps are taken, the horse is likely to work quite happily when he is put to again.

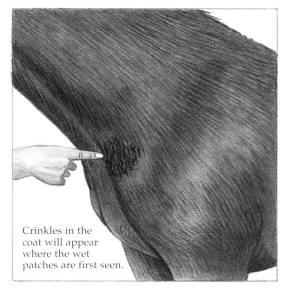

Crinkles in the coat will appear where the wet patches are first seen.

The approximate area of the shoulder that is usually rubbed by a dirty or ill-fitting full collar or by too much work by an unfit animal.

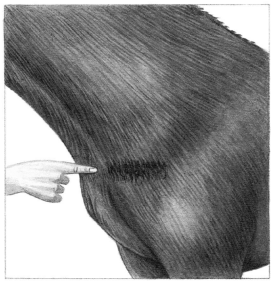

Area which is most commonly rubbed if a breast collar is used with fixed trace hooks instead of a swingle tree.

Fear of traffic

It really is not safe to drive on modern roads an animal who is frightened of traffic. It is therefore essential to traffic proof young horses so that the problem is prevented.

It is wise to get the use of a roadside field in which the youngster can be turned out and constantly see and hear heavy traffic and farm machinery. It is not a good idea to turn him out with a companion who is nervous because they are likely to frighten each other and gallop away every time that something large appears. Ideally he should be put with an animal which is immune to heavy traffic. Of course it is vital that the fencing is of hedging or timber so that dangers are lessened.

Having spent several months in such a field, the horse is much less likely to be afraid of traffic when he is ridden or driven on the roads. This method is far more satisfactory than trying to take the youngster for walks along roads where fast moving heavy traffic may be met. It takes a handler with very strong nerves and arms to cope with a youngster leaping about on the end of a rein every time a large or noisy vehicle appears. Such tactics can actually make an animal worse in traffic.

When the youngster is first taken out on the roads, it is a great help if he can be accompanied by a thoroughly traffic proof animal so that he can follow by example.

Before venturing onto public roads it is essential to ensure that you have adequate third-party insurance. It is also advisable that the turnout should be easily seen. Bright clothes and/or a suitable tabard are a help.

An effective and simple method of helping to make horses traffic proof.

A simple turning point to give a purpose to a short drive out and back.

Driving in company

When the Whip gains confidence in his turnout, thoughts often turn to the possibility of going out in company or perhaps to a show or event.

Before embarking on showing or eventing it is sensible to take the animal out in company to a rally or similar outing which is properly organised by a driving society. This will enable the horse to see other turnouts before having to face the electric atmosphere of a show. His driver is also likely to be more relaxed at a rally, which will be advantageous for all concerned.

Before going to a rally, it is very important to accustom the horse to the sight and sound of another horse in harness. It is sensible to drive out with another turnout and take it in turns to drive in front and then behind.

When the opportunity permits, it is a good idea to drive side by side, which is the most frightening for a harness horse. He is able to hear the other turnout but is not able to see it because of his blinkers. The time and trouble spent doing this simple schooling is worth every moment. Then, when the horse is faced with several turnouts at a rally he is far less likely to become frightened. The confidence which has been gained by the driver during the training sessions, will be transmitted to the horse to mutual advantage.

It is sensible to tell the organiser of the rally that this is your first outing. It will be a help if you can follow an experienced Whip with a mature animal.

It is important to take an active groom to assist if a problem should arise. You must not expect the drivers of other vehicles to abandon their grooms in order to help you out of a muddle.

DRIVING IN COMPANY

Refusing to stand still

Some horses are very disobedient about standing still while they are being put to or while the vehicle is being mounted. They try to rush off as soon as the Whip puts a foot onto the mounting step, or, in extreme cases, as soon as the reins are picked up. Such an animal is dangerous and must be restrained. He needs to be taken 'back to basics'.

He must learn to be obedient and respectful. The best method is to go back to work, on the lunge, in an enclosed school where he must be taught to halt, walk and trot on both reins on command by voice. The word 'whoa' must be taught to mean 'stand where you are and do not move until I tell you that you may'.

I am a believer in titbits for training some animals. This does, of course, depend on the temperament as some horses just cannot be given titbits because it makes them bite. It does not usually take long to teach a horse to halt on command. He will usually halt once he understands what is required. I then repeat the work with the horse in open bridle, driving saddle, crupper and long reins, still on a circle of about 30 metres.

HALT ON LONG-REINS

WORKING ON THE LUNGE

HALT ON THE LONG REINS

We then go for walks and halt from time to time being sure to reward either verbally or with a titbit when the halt is properly established.

Gradually, the titbits are reduced until they are not given at all. I then get the horse used to facing a garage type door and get him to stand, unheld. At this stage he has gained confidence and the blinkered bridle can be put on instead of the open bridle and the previous work is repeated. I ask him to stand facing the door until he is told to walk on and come round.

When he is thoroughly obedient and calm he can be put to the vehicle in this position and, with luck, he will stand still until he is told that he can come round. It will not be long before he dwells while I mount and waits patiently before walking on when asked to do so.

Failure to spend time in retraining at the early stages of this bad habit will almost certainly result in an accident one day. It is well worth spending the time that it may take to cure the appallingly bad habit of rushing off.

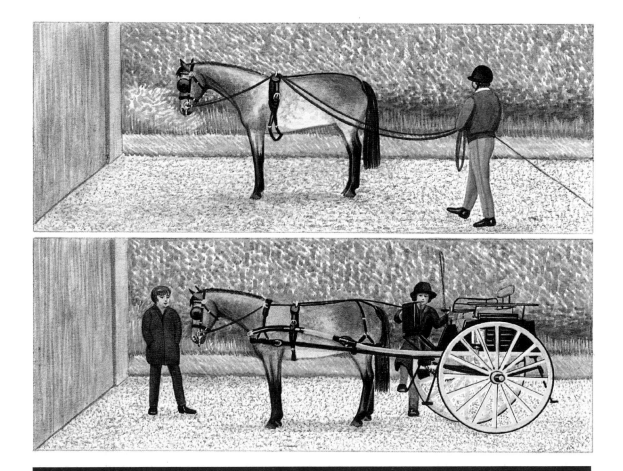

Pulling

Some horses, who are normally quiet and calm at home, will hot up and pull when they are driven in company. It is very important to ensure that the bitting is comfortable.

Many will pull by opening their mouths wide and crossing their jaws. It is usually better to tighten the noseband or add a flash or Grakle noseband in order to prevent the mouth from being opened wide, than to put the reins onto the bottom bar of the Liverpool bit. Just putting the reins onto the bottom bar will probably result in the horse pulling even harder with his mouth wide open and jaw firmly crossed. His mouth will become deadened and his chin groove may become calloused. The situation is likely to get worse at every outing.

Obviously, if the reins have been buckled onto the plain cheek position, then putting them onto rough cheek or upper bar, as well as attending to the opening of the mouth and crossing of the jaw, will help to solve the problem.

Many horses prefer a low-port mouthpiece which allows the tongue to lie in the arch. This also helps to prevent an animal getting his tongue over the bit, which can be another evasion.

The resistance of crossing the jaws and opening the mouth is a common fault.

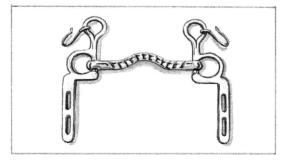

Elbow bit with a low port to accommodate the tongue. The shape of the cheeks prevents the horse from catching hold of the cheeks with his lips.

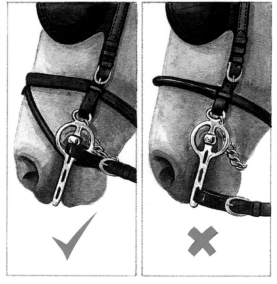

Reins on rough cheek together with a flash noseband prevent the jaw being crossed and opened wide. The reins on bottom bar might not be as effective.

Eventing

Interest in horse driving trials is increasing. It is possible to compete, at club level, in all three phases – dressage and presentation, cross country, and cones – with the same vehicle. It is wise to get a modern vehicle on carriage-type wheels, which has been built specially for the purpose. This will then be of the correct weight and width for the class.

Most vehicles are now made to enable the groom to stand on the back step, which is far safer than being seated beside the driver when going across country. Many of the two-wheelers can be adjusted for balance depending on whether the groom is on the seat beside the driver or on the rear step. Some people favour four-wheelers for driving single animals across country, claiming that they are more stable.

Many newcomers own just one vehicle and need to use it for everyday exercising as well as for competing. The main problem here lies in having to get the cart clean enough for presentation and dressage whilst having to use it for exercising on the day before an event. There is so much to prepare with the horse and the harness that last-minute cleaning of a vehicle can be stressful.

The training for horse driving trials is similar to that for ridden events. A great deal of that which applies to ridden dressage also is applicable to driven dressage. Training under saddle and on long reins is important to get the necessary results in harness.

The cross-country course and the cones course have to be given similar consideration as ridden cross country and show jumping. Many of the same things apply to driving trials in the way in which the courses must be walked and studied for the best routes to take.

CONES

DRESSAGE

CROSS COUNTRY

Showing considered

If the ambition is to compete in showing classes then a high-class carriage which is suitable for the animal and Whip concerned will have to be obtained if success is to be achieved at top level.

If the horse is fine and elegant then he should be put to a vehicle which is also fine and elegant.

A hackney to a Spider Phaeton can look superb.

A Welsh Cob of substance would look heavy in such a carriage and be more suited to a heavier gig or Dog cart (right).

The size and shape of the Whip also has to be considered. A large person driving a small pony will not look as elegant as a small person driving a similar turnout.

A neatly dressed large person can look smart driving a pair of ponies because the vehicle which is used will be larger and probably have more leg room.

TANDEM

UNICORN

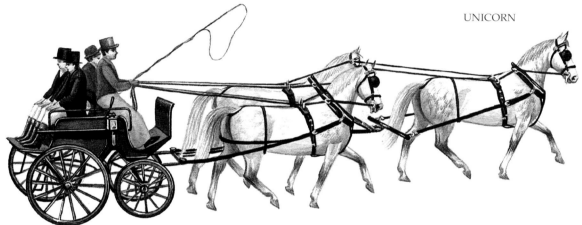

Different showing classes call for different types of carriages.

Country cart classes are often won by Whips driving varnished vehicles with horses in brown harness. Dog carts and vehicles of that type are most favoured.

Pairs, unicorns and teams can be driven to Phaetons, Dog carts and Breaks.

Tandems look best in high two wheeled vehicles which give the Whip a clear view over their leader's head.

Concours d'Elégance classes, as the name suggests, are for the most elegant equipage. This is usually judged by an artist who chooses the turnout which he or she would most like to paint.

CONCOURS D'ELEGANCE

Conclusion

As with all production and training of horses it is dedication, patience and attention to detail which usually result in success. A driving horse will only be able to give maximum pleasure if he is comfortable in his harness and vehicle. Just as important is careful training so that he understands, thoroughly, what he is meant to be doing.

It is important to remember that it takes years, not weeks, to produce a high-class and confident driving animal. The result is well worth the time and trouble which one must spend.

An obedient horse is usually a happy horse and such an animal is likely to give the whole family pleasure for many years.